NATIONS IN THE NEWS

Republic of
Georgia

By Charles Piddock

Academic Consultant: Jay Bergman
Professor of History
Central Connecticut State University
New Britain, Connecticut

WORLD ALMANAC® LIBRARY

Please visit our Web site at: www.garethstevens.com
For a free color catalog describing World Almanac® Library's list of high-quality books and multimedia programs, call 1-800-848-2928 (USA) or 1-800-387-3178 (Canada).
World Almanac® Library's fax: (414) 332-3567

Library of Congress Catalog-in-Publication Data

Piddock, Charles.
    Republic of Georgia / by Charles Piddock.
        p. cm. — (Nations in the news)
    Includes bibliographical references and index.
    ISBN-10: 0-8368-6710-6 — ISBN-13: 978-0-8368-6710-7 (lib. bdg.)
    ISBN-10: 0-8368-6717-3 — ISBN-13: 978-0-8368-6717-6 (softcover)
    1. Georgia (Republic)—History—Juvenile literature. I. Title.
II. Series: Piddock, Charles. Nations in the news.
    DK675.6.P53   2006
    947.58—dc22   2006011935

First published in 2007 by
World Almanac® Library
A Member of the WRC Media Family of Companies
330 West Olive Street, Suite 100
Milwaukee, WI 53132 USA

A Creative Media Applications, Inc. Production
Design and Production: Alan Barnett, Inc.
Editor: Susan Madoff
Copy Editor: Laurie Lieb
Proofreaders: Laurie Lieb and Donna Drybread
Indexer: Nara Wood
World Almanac® Library editorial direction: Mark J. Sachner
World Almanac® Library editor: Gini Holland
World Almanac® Library art direction: Tammy West
World Almanac® Library production: Jessica Morris

Photo credits: Landov: cover photo, page 39; Associated Press: pages 5, 7, 8, 11, 22, 26, 29, 31, 32, 34, 35, 37, 39, 40, 42; New York Public Library, Astor, Lenox and Tilden Foundations: pages 12, 19; Northwind Pictures Archive: page 14; Bridgeman Art Library: pages 16, 17, 18; Library of Congress: page 20; Getty Images: page 23; maps courtesy of Ortelius Design.

Printed in the United States of America

1 2 3 4 5 6 7 8 9 10 09 08 07 06

Table of Contents

Cover photo : A parade marking the end of training for Georgian Special Forces soldiers by U.S. instructors is held at Republic Square in Tbilisi, Georgia, in April 2004.

CHAPTER 1

The Struggle for Unity

O n May 10, 2005, U.S. president George W. Bush was far from home. He had gone halfway around the world to Tbilisi, capital of the Republic of Georgia. Tens of thousands of people jammed into Freedom Square in Tbilisi to hear the president speak.

When he appeared before the huge crowd, President Bush got one of the warmest receptions of his presidency. He opened by praising Georgia's

The Republic of Georgia is located in southwestern Asia and is bordered by Russia in the north and east; Turkey, Armenia, and Azerbaijan to the south; and the Black Sea to the west. The rugged terrain of the Caucasus Mountains separates the country from the Russian Federation, and Georgia controls most of the routes through the mountain range.

In Freedom Square in Tbilisi, Georgia, in May 2005, U.S. president George W. Bush spoke of his admiration for the people of Georgia and the inspiration they provide to people in oppressed regimes all over the world.

"Rose Revolution," the uprising of November 2003 that overthrew a corrupt government without a single act of violence—an achievement rarely seen in world history. "You gathered here [in this square]," the president told the cheering crowd, "armed with nothing but roses and [the] power of your convictions, and you claimed your liberty. And because you acted,

Georgia today is both [self-governing] and free and a beacon of liberty for this region and the world."

The U.S. president received the most thunderous applause and loudest cheers when he told the crowd, "The **sovereignty** and territorial integrity of Georgia must be respected…by *all* nations." The words *sovereignty* and *territorial integrity* had very specific meanings to Georgians who heard them in 2005. They continue to have strong meaning today. They were aimed at Russia, which Georgia fears is trying to encourage **breakaway** parts of the country to separate from Georgia and become part of Russia. The president's visit to Georgia marked his attempt to send a signal to Russia that the United States supports Georgia's territorial integrity and right to run its own affairs.

Two Breakaway Regions

The United States and the Georgian government are concerned about Russia's support of the Georgian regions of Abkhazia and South Ossetia. **Separatists** in both regions look upon Russia as their protector against Georgia's attempts to reestablish control. Georgia's president, Mikhail Saakashvili, has vowed to defeat the separatists and to reclaim both regions. Saakashvili and other Georgian politicians see Russia as a roadblock to national unity. All three areas—Georgia, Abkhazia, South Ossetia—and the other nations of the Caucasus Mountain region were once part of the Russian Empire. They were later a part of the Union of Soviet Socialist Republics (USSR), or Soviet Union, the huge communist nation that replaced the Russian Empire.

"A lot of politicians in Russia still have imperial ambitions and an imperial mentality. They don't want to lose Georgia as a sphere of interest and influence," said Nino Burzhadnadze, the Speaker of Georgia's parliament, in March 2006. "They think that in the interests of Russia they should have a sick and disintegrated Georgia, which will be quite easy to manipulate, and in this way to have some influence in the Caucasus [region]."

The Heart of the Caucasus

Georgia is a country slightly smaller in area than South Carolina. It is located in Asia in the heart of the Caucasus Mountains on the coast of the Black Sea. Georgia is often called "strategic," or important to other countries, because of its location. Georgia borders Azerbaijan, Armenia, and Turkey on the south. On the north, the snow-capped Caucasus Mountains divide Georgia from its giant Russian neighbor.

Georgia controls most of the routes through the Caucasus Mountains and the mountains themselves.

Georgia's population is 4.6 million. Most of the people are Georgians, an ancient people who have lived on the same land for thousands of years. Georgians make up 70.1 percent of the country's population. Significant minorities include Armenian (8.1 percent), Russian (6.1 percent), Azeri (5.7 percent), Ossetian (3 percent), and Abkhazian (1.8 percent). The remaining 5 percent is made up of a number of smaller **ethnic** groups. Despite the overwhelming majority of Georgians in Georgia as a whole, a number of non-Georgian ethnic groups, particularly the Abkhazians and Ossetians, are heavily concentrated in specific areas of the country—Abkhazia and South Ossetia—where they have lived for centuries.

When the Soviet Union collapsed in 1991, order inside the newly independent nation of Georgia collapsed as well. Although Georgia's constitu-

FAST FACT

The collapse of the Soviet Union produced fifteen new countries: the Baltic nations of Estonia, Lithuania, and Latvia; the Eastern European nations of Russia, Ukraine, Belarus, and Moldova; the Central Asian nations of Kazakhstan, Kyrgyzstan, Tajikistan, Uzbekistan, and Turkmenistan; and the Caucasus Mountains nations of Georgia, Armenia, and Azerbaijan.

Peacekeeping troops monitor the village of Eredvi, Georgia, in South Ossetia in August 2004, amid fears that fighting in the region might lead to full-scale warfare.

tion gave Abkhazia and South Ossetia self-rule, they rejected Georgian rule and declared themselves to be independent countries.

South Ossetia

South Ossetia was first to declare itself independent. This mountainous region is separated from North Ossetia, which is part of Russia, by the Georgian-Russian border that runs high in the Caucasus.

The Ossetians, who number only about seventy thousand, are descended from tribes who migrated to the area many centuries ago from farther east in Asia, near Iran. They speak a language related to Farsi, the Persian language of Iran today. Georgians account for less than one-third of South Ossetia's population.

For hundreds of years, the Ossetians have had good relations with the Russians and have wanted to be a part of Russia, not Georgia. Russia always regarded them as loyal citizens. Under Soviet Georgia, South Ossetia had a large degree of self-rule. The region had its own president and regional parliament. In December 1990, shortly before the collapse of the Soviet Union, Georgian leader Zviad Gamsakhurdia took away South Ossetia's self-rule.

In reaction, the South Ossetian **legislature** declared that the region was separating from Georgia and uniting with North Ossetia inside Russia. Georgian forces then invaded South Ossetia. Hundreds died in the fighting and thousands of **refugees** fled both parts of Ossetia. There has been a **stalemate** ever since, with Georgia demanding that South Ossetia stay inside Georgia, and the South Ossetians demanding union with North Ossetia. Russian troops remain in South Ossetia, as "**peacekeepers**," say the Ossetians, but Georgia says they are there to help the separatists.

As a result of the conflict, South Ossetia's **infrastructure**—its roads, bridges and other public structures—remains nearly destroyed. The economy is also in shambles, with crime and smuggling reportedly one of the few ways to make money.

Mountain Face-off

When Mikhail Saakashvili was elected president of Georgia in 2004, he offered to restore South Ossetian self-rule within Georgia. The separatists refused, demanding complete separation from Georgia. In May 2004 South Ossetia held parliamentary elections, which Georgia refused to recognize. Soon afterward, Georgia moved troops up to the South Ossetia border. In August, fighting broke out between Georgian soldiers and South Ossetian separatist forces. Both sides, however, soon agreed to a **cease-fire**.

South Ossetia's separatists are hoping for support from Russia. Although the Georgian parliament has called for their withdrawal, Russia still has peacekeeping forces there. While Russia does not officially recognize South

Georgian president Mikhail Saakashvili delivers a speech in Marneuli, 25 miles (40 km) east of Tbilisi on March 21, 2006, in honor of the national holiday of Navruz, which celebrates the arrival of spring. He is surrounded by children wearing traditional costumes.

Ossetia's independence, it maintains close contacts with separatist leaders.

The president of South Ossetia is Eduard Kokoity, who won unrecognized presidential elections in December 2001. He has angered Georgia by stating that his aim is the **unification** of North and South Ossetia within Russia. He has warned Saakashvili against aggressive Georgian **nationalism**. He also insists that the people of South Ossetia do not regard themselves as part of Georgia.

Trouble in Abkhazia

The second major conflict threatening Georgian unity concerns a region known as Abkhazia. Abkhazia is located in the northwest corner of Georgia. The Black Sea lies to its southwest, the Caucasus Mountains and Russia to its north.

During the time that Georgia was part of the Russian Empire (1801–1917) and the Soviet Union (1921–1991), Abkhazia was a favorite vacation place for wealthy Russians. It had warm weather along the coast, great beaches, and, further inland, pine forests and snow-capped mountains. Although the Abkhazians are an ancient people with their own language and culture, Russian and Georgian, were the region's official languages, not Abkhazian. Many Georgians and Russians settled inside Abkhazia.

In 1993 Abkhazia declared itself independent of Georgia. Heavy fighting between Georgian troops and Abkhazian separatists erupted. The better-armed Georgian troops managed to gain control of most of Abkhazia. The separatists, however, were able to mount a counterattack and push the Georgian forces back from Abkhazia. The Georgians accused the Russians of helping the Abkhazians win the war.

More than ten thousand people died in the Abkhazian war. Significant **"ethnic cleansing"**—the forced removal of an ethnic group—also caused hardship. Abkhazians pushed almost the entire Georgian population of Abkhazia—over 250,000 people— out of the region. Many of those Georgians had deep roots in Abkhazia, some going back hundreds of years. Their homes and property were confiscated by Abkhazians or left to rot.

When the last Soviet census of Abkhazia was taken in 1989, the region had a population of 500,000. Forty-eight percent were Georgian, and 17 percent were Abkhazian. Today, Abkhazia's total population is only 250,000. Abkhazians make up the largest group—48 percent. The rest— 52 percent—consists of Russians, Georgians, and others.

Today, Abkhazia considers itself an independent country. It has its own president and legislature. No other country, however, including Russia, which has close ties with Abkhazia, has recognized Abkhazia's independence.

Abkhazia and the government of Georgia are still officially at war, although no major fighting has taken place recently. The fragile peace is kept by two separate peacekeeping forces. One is from the **United Nations (UN)** and one is chiefly composed of Russian troops.

Bitterness and Revenge

The Abkhazian conflict left a strong legacy of bitterness and a desire for revenge on both sides. "Our presence here is important," Major Yusuf El-Bdour of the UN peacekeeping force told the British Broadcasting Corporation (BBC) in 2005. "The locals feel that they are safe when they see the UN cars and the UN flag. If we leave I think the conflict will begin from the beginning." Major El-Bdour's patrol often drives past old, beautiful houses left by fleeing Georgians more than ten years ago and now falling down.

In Georgia, Georgians displaced from Abkhazia by the war still wait to go home. "If Abkhazians don't want to let us return peacefully," a Georgian named Georgi told a reporter, "we'll go anyway by force. I want my house back. I want to see the grave of my father and my nephew. How long can

we wait? One way or another we have to go back."

Abkhazia, however, says there will be no homecoming unless Georgia recognizes Abkhazia's complete independence. "There is no way we will reunite with Georgia," Abkhazian prime minister Raul Hadzhimba told the BBC, "not after all the lives that have been lost."

Abkhazia's economy was ruined by the war and has not recovered. It is kept functioning only through Russian support, through a single road across the Russian-Abkhazian border. Georgia claims that Russia is busy extending its influence in Abkhazia, part of a plan to make the region part of Russia and to dismember and weaken Georgia.

Georgia has asked for the complete removal of Russian peacekeepers and military bases from Abkhazia. By early April 2006, tensions between the two countries over Abkhazia remained high.

Headed for War?

The United States has strongly supported the Georgian government's effort to unite Georgia. The United States, however, wants unification to take place peacefully. Previous Georgian president Eduard Shevardnadze had hoped that, over time and with the help of Russia, Georgia would be reunited. The separatist movements, however, have gotten stronger over time, not weaker. Many of the residents of Abkhazia and South Ossetia have also received Russian citizenship, and Russia has pledged to protect its new citizens.

Georgian president Saakashvili has promised that Georgia will be reunited during his term as president. Eduard Kokoity, president of the separatist republic of South Ossetia, says it will never happen. "We have nothing in common with Georgia," he maintains.

"Soon, the Kremlin will have to make a fateful decision about what to do with Georgia. Moscow will either have to help its citizens living in Abkhazia and South Ossetia or pretend that it does not notice Georgia's aggression," said a commentator on Russian television in March 2006.

A conflict with Russia would ruin Georgia economically. Despite the economic costs, Georgian society and thousands of refugees from Abkhazia and South Ossetia have been urging Georgia's president to make good on his preelection promises.

Just how sensitive relations between Georgia and Russia have become was apparent in January 2006 in the midst of a bitter cold spell. On January 21 several explosions ripped through the main natural gas supply pipeline from Russia to Armenia and Georgia. Both countries relied on natural gas for heat, and, with the temperature well below

President Eduard Kokoity of the separatist region of South Ossetia speaks at a news conference in Moscow in June 2004, repeating his call for unification of South Ossetia with Russia.

zero, tempers heated up. President Saakashvili accused Russia of deliberately blowing up the pipeline to punish Georgia. The Russians said the bombers were Chechen rebels, who are at war with Russia. Chechnya, a Russian province directly north of Georgia, has been the scene of a violent civil war between separatists and Russian forces. After a frigid week, however, natural gas was again flowing into Georgia from Russia and from Iran.

CHAPTER 2

An Ancient Land

Georgia is truly an ancient land. Cave drawings discovered by **archaeologists** along the Black Sea coast suggest that humans lived there 150,000 years ago, during the Old Stone Age. These early Georgians survived by hunting and supplemented their diets by gathering fruits and berries. By 5000 B.C. people in Georgia lived in villages and hunted and fished for food. They also began to grow grain. Archaeologists know this because they have found stone sickles and other primitive farm tools.

This photo is of the monastery in Mtskheta, one of Georgia's oldest cities and the former capital of the Georgian kingdom of Iberia from the third to the fifth century B.C. Mtskheta is still the headquarters of the Georgian Orthodox and Apostolic Church.

About 3000 B.C. Georgians developed the skills to produce bronze weapons and tools. Bronze is a metal made by combining tin and copper. It proved much stronger than copper or tin alone, making sharper and better tools and weapons. About 2100 B.C. a people called the Kurgans invaded the Caucasus from the vast steppes, or grasslands, to the north. The Kurgans intermarried with the people already in Georgia to form what is now called the Trialeti culture, centered in a region southwest of modern Tbilisi. It was about this time that Georgian skill in metalwork became the most renowned in the ancient world. Burial mounds dating from 2100 B.C. to 1500 B.C. reveal the power and wealth of Trialeti chieftains. Many of the tombs contain drinking cups and plates of finely crafted gold and silver.

Colchis and Greece

The first written records of the tribes and rulers of Georgia come from the **annals** of the Assyrians. The Assyrians came from what is now northern Iraq. They conquered an empire that by the ninth century B.C. stretched from what is now Israel to Iran and as far north as the mountains of eastern Turkey.

The western part of Georgia, known as Colchis, became well known to the early Greeks, who by the eighth century B.C. had set up colonies and trading stations all around the Black Sea. Colchis became famous in both history and in mythology as the fabulously wealthy homeland of Medea and the Golden Fleece.

About 730 B.C. the Cimmerians and Scythians, nomads from the grasslands of the north, attacked and occupied much of the Caucasus region, including Colchis. They pushed out the native Georgian tribes, who sought refuge in the mountains. Two native tribes, the Tibareni and the Muski, however, managed to reestablish themselves in what was to become eastern Georgia by the fourth century B.C. They then merged to form the kingdom of Iberia (not to be confused with the Latin name for Spain and Portugal), with its capital at Mtskheta, about 20 miles (32 kilometers) north of modern-day Tbilisi. It was at Mtskheta that a common Georgian language was developed. Mtskheta thrived and grew wealthy because it was part of the Silk Road, a series of overland trade routes that linked Europe and the Middle East with India and China. In 66 B.C. Iberia became part of the Roman Empire after being conquered by the legions commanded by the Roman general Pompey. Roman civilization brought new roads and increased trade between Colchis and the rest of the vast Roman Empire.

The story of the Golden Fleece is one of the most famous tales to come us from ancient Greece. According to the tale, Jason was a Greek prince whose father had lost his throne to Pelias, Jason's uncle. Jason could regain the throne only by finding a fabulous fleece (the skin of a sheep) made of gold. Bravely undertaking the quest, Jason and a band of fifty men sailed toward Colchis in a ship called the *Argo*, from which they took the name Argonauts.

After many harrowing and exciting adventures in their voyage across the sea, the Argonauts finally reached Colchis in western present-day Georgia. The king of Colchis, however, refused to give up the fleece unless Jason proved himself by passing several trials of strength and intelligence. First, Jason had to tame the king's fire-snorting bulls and yoke them to plow. Jason, who was both strong and smart, soon had the massive beasts yoked to the plow.

The next trial required Jason to plow a field with the bulls and plant a helmetful of dragon's teeth. Once in the ground, each tooth was to spring up into an armed warrior, whom Jason had to defeat by arms. This time Jason needed help, and he got it from Medea, the king's daughter, who was a **sorcerer**. Medea advised Jason to throw stones among the somewhat dimwitted warriors, who turned in anger upon each other and fought to the death, leaving Jason victorious.

The king, however, still refused to part with the fleece, which was guarded by an ever-watchful dragon. Once again, Medea came to Jason's aid by guiding him to the fleece and casting a spell on the dragon, putting it to sleep. Jason then escaped in the *Argo* with both the fleece and Medea.

The story of Jason and the Golden Fleece was long thought to be pure myth, but some experts suggest that the Argonauts' journey may actually have had a basis in fact. Colchis was a fabulously wealthy land ruled by powerful kings. Prospectors in the region once known as Colchis were found to have used sheepskins to trap fine gold particles in the rivers that flowed from the mountains. They would then dry the skins and beat out their golden contents.

Conversion to Christianity

At the time of the Roman Empire, the Iberians were considered a brave, warlike people with a proud tradition as fighters. They had their own fierce tribal gods. In A.D. 330, during the reign of the Roman emperor Constantine the Great, the Iberians converted to Christianity. The conversion of Iberia is attributed to Saint Nino, a woman who was said to have miraculous healing powers. At the time, the Roman Empire also controlled Armenia, which had converted to Christianity thirty years before, becoming the first nation in the world to do so.

Political conditions at the time also favored the adoption of Christianity since it was now the official creed of the Roman Empire. Christians found themselves favored for jobs and official appointments.

In the 400s King Vakhtan Gorgasali strengthened the new Iberian church by establishing a bishop independent of the king. The bishop's palace was at Mtskheta, which remains the center of the Georgian Orthodox Church today. King Gorgasali also founded Tbilisi in 458, making it his capital.

On the western side of Iberia lay Lazica, a Georgian kingdom that had sprung up in the area of ancient Colchis. Lazica adopted Christianity in the sixth century. For much of the sixth and seventh centuries, both Georgian kingdoms found themselves at the center of a power struggle between two great powers. One was the Byzantine Empire (the empire that succeeded the Roman Empire) to the west. The other was the kingdom of Persia to the east. Both empires seemed to take turns controlling events in Georgia. The struggle ended when the Arabs, inspired by the new religion of Islam, swept through Persia and captured Tbilisi in 645.

Arab Domination

The Arabs, who were busy conquering other parts of the world, were not especially interested in turning Georgia into an Arab country. They allowed the Georgians to practice

Christianity and Georgian culture without interference. Georgian rulers were allowed to rule, but under the control of an Arab emir, or ruler.

By the ninth century, Arab influence on much of Georgia outside of Tbilisi had declined and a native **dynasty**, the Bagratids, came to power. This remarkable family of kings and queens was to hold power in Georgia for the next thousand years. The dynasty ended only when Georgia became part of the Russian Empire in 1801.

The first Bagratid ruler in Georgia was Ashot I (780–826), who came from a prominent family in Armenia. Ashot ruled under the authority of the Byzantine emperor. Since both the Byzantine Empire and the Arab rulers were weak at this time, Ashot was effectively an independent king in southern and western Georgia.

King Bagrat III (960–1014) also became king of the Abkhazians, unifying the eastern and western parts of Georgia for the first time. During his rule Georgia established many of the same borders it has today. Tbilisi, however, was still controlled by the Arabs during Bagrat's rule. Under Bagrat IV (1018–1072), Georgia emerged as one of the most powerful states in the Caucasus.

David the Builder

Giorgi III, the son of Bagrat IV, was faced with a new challenge: the

David the Builder (in solid red robe) of the Bagratid Dynasty is illustrated along with other royalty and Catholic priests from the Armenian Church in this ancient drawing.

Georgia's greatest poet is Shota Rustaveli (*shown left*) (1172–1216), who lived during the reign of Queen Tamar. Rustaveli's most famous poem is *The Knight in the Panther's Skin,* the Georgian national epic. The poem tells the story of a knight's passionate search for a woman who symbolizes the Sun and who has been stolen by another knight and taken to the West, across the sea. The poem celebrates human qualities such as love, friendship, courage, and strength. Rustaveli's brave, generous heroes symbolize ideals of human behavior.

Little is known of Rustaveli's early life. According to legend, he was orphaned as a child and brought up by an uncle who was a Christian monk. Rustaveli later wrote a series of poems in honor of Queen Tamar. As a reward, the queen appointed him her court treasurer. Georgian traditions say that the poet fell in love with the queen.

Muslim Seljuk Turks. The Seljuks had captured Persia and Armenia and pushed westward, invading the Byzantine Empire. They crushed the Byzantine army at the Battle of Manzikert in 1071. Giorgi III was unable to deal with the threat posed by the Seljuks, so he gave up his throne to his sixteen-year-old son, David, who was crowned David IV (1073–1125).

David, known in Georgian history as David the Builder, became one of Georgia's greatest rulers. David restored order to the country and slowly pushed the Seljuks out of its border regions, winning battle after battle with them. The victories added to the reputation of Georgians as tough, ruthless fighters—a reputation that has lasted to modern times. David also recaptured Tbilisi from the Arabs and Turks. He extended Georgia's territory as far as the Caspian Sea and captured parts of Armenia as well. David is also revered in Georgia for the many monasteries, churches, and schools he had built. Today he is honored as a saint of the Georgian Orthodox Church.

The great works of David IV were continued by his great-granddaughter, Queen Tamar (1160–1213). During her rule, Georgian feudal society reached its high point in culture, art, and literature. The virtues of chivalry and honor at the court of Tamar were celebrated in an epic romance, *The Knight in the Panther's Skin*, by Shota Rustaveli. The queen's reign is still considered Georgia's golden age.

An invasion of the Caucasus in 1220 brought this golden age to a sudden end. Led by Genghis Khan, the **Mongols** erupted out of Mongolia to conquer a vast empire stretching from China to the borders of Europe. Queen Tamar's heir, King Giorgi IV Lasha (1192–1223), was killed in bat-

A print of a fresco shows Queen Tamar and her father, King Giorgi III, whose reigns are remembered for their refined ideals and culture.

tle against the Mongols, who dominated Georgia for the next century, taxing the Georgians heavily. King Giorgi V (reigned 1286–1346), called "The Brilliant," regained Georgia's independence briefly until another Mongol conqueror, Tamerlane (1336–1405), overran Georgia. Tamerlane's army plundered Georgia eight times. As a result, much of the country was ruined and much of the population fled into the mountains.

For the next three centuries, Georgia was ruled by native kings, but they were controlled by Muslim Persia (modern-day Iran). Under Persian rule, Georgians were persecuted for their Christian beliefs. The Persians also deported many Georgians to distant parts of Persia, where their descendants can still be found today.

Enter the Russians

In the early 1700s Persian power began to decline, allowing the kings of Georgia to get a measure of their authority back. A new power, however, was expanding rapidly in the Caucasus region: Russia.

At this time, Persian-backed Muslim raiders made constant attacks on Georgia, crippling the nation's trade and industry. It is estimated that Georgia may have lost half its

Alexander I, Emperor of All Russias, is shown in uniform, ready for battle.

population to these raids. King Herekle II (1720–1798) believed that his Christian nation could not long hold out against the attacks. He sought the aid of Christian Russia. In 1783, Russia and Georgia signed the Treaty of Georgievsk. Under the agreement, Georgia agreed to become a Russian **protectorate**. Despite the treaty, a Persian army took Tbilisi in 1795 and slaughtered fifty thousand of its inhabitants.

In 1800, Herekle's son, King Giorgi XII, decided to turn the kingdom over to the Russians completely in exchange for their protection. That same year, he died. He was the last ruler of the thousand-year-old Bagratid dynasty. In 1801, the Russian czar Alexander I confirmed that Georgia was a part of the Russian empire. He officially abolished the Bagratid dynasty. Georgian kings were replaced by Russian military governors.

CHAPTER 3

Czars and Communists

Despite several early popular uprisings in Georgia, Russian rule brought stability to Georgia. Prince Michael Vorontsov (1782–1856) was the first Russian **viceroy** in Georgia. Vorontsov deeply respected Georgian traditions, and the Georgians learned to trust and like him. Georgia's economy, now safe from Persian raids, prospered.

In 1872, the Russians built a railway linking Tbilisi with the town of Poti. Factories, mines, and plantations were also developed with Russian and European money. Georgia was becoming a modern nation. Russian and European culture and education replaced old Georgian ideas, at least in the cities. Russian, instead of Georgian, was taught in the schools.

Russian Cossacks living in the southern steppe regions of Russia gather on horseback. These skilled horsemen, used by the czar to guard state and ethnic boundaries, fought for Russia in wars throughout the eighteenth and nineteenth centuries.

Students were required to read Russian writers instead of Georgian writers. Modern science replaced the old religious education. Much of the countryside, however, was more like the American Wild West than settled Europe. Often justice or revenge was settled by gunshot. Black markets and smuggling, a Georgian tradition, continued and grew. Georgian traditions of clan, family, and ethnic loyalties ran deep. Throughout the Russian empire, Georgians were known as a tough people who were dangerous to anger or double-cross. Georgians still have such a reputation today.

Many Georgian **intellectuals** reacted against Russian influence. The "Men of the '60s" in nineteenth-century Tbilisi were a group of **radicals** and social activists, full of the new social democratic ideals of equality then current in Europe. The 1890s saw the appearance of another group of radicals advocating revolution who had absorbed the political ideas of Karl Marx while studying abroad. Marx (1818–1883) was the founder of **communism**. The leader of this communist group in Georgia was Noe Zhordania (1868–1953). Another prominent member was Joseph Dzhugashvili. Dzhugashvili, under his adopted name of Joseph Stalin, was later to become a ruthless Soviet dictator.

War and Revolution

In 1905, unrest over harsh working conditions led to protests and industrial strikes throughout the Russian empire, including Georgia. The government of Czar Nicholas II (1868–1918) used Cossacks, a warlike people of southern Russia who fought in the czar's army, to put down strikes and demonstrations with heavy loss of life.

In 1914, Russia entered World War I (1914–1918) against Germany and Austro-Hungary. The war did not go well for the czar. In 1917, after a series of defeats, the Russian army collapsed. The collapse was followed in November 1917 by the Russian Revolution, followed by a communist uprising. Under the leadership of Vladimir Lenin (1870–1924), the communists seized power from the revolutionary government that had replaced the czar.

Joseph Stalin was born in Gori, Georgia, on December 18, 1878. His father was a peasant who worked in a shoe factory. He was also a drunkard who beat his wife and small son. One of Stalin's boyhood friends said that the boy took the beatings without crying, proving he was as tough and "as heartless as his father."

As a boy, Stalin was fascinated by Georgian folklore. The stories he read told of Georgian mountain men who fought for Georgian independence.

Stalin attended a religious college. His interests there, however, quickly turned from religion to revolution. As a convert to communism, he joined a Georgian group advocating a communist revolution. Stalin gave up his birth name of Joseph Vissarionovich and adopted the name Stalin, from the Russian word for "steel." He became the communists' "man of steel."

Stalin became active in Georgia's revolutionary underground. He was arrested and imprisoned many times and exiled to Siberia twice by the czarist authorities. His friendship with Vladimir Lenin, the leader of the Russian communists, put him near the forefront of the 1917 Bolshevik revolution that brought the communists to power. When Lenin died in 1924, Stalin had enough power to disgrace his political rivals. In 1928 he exiled his main political rival, Leon Trotsky (1879–1940). He had now gained absolute control of the Communist Party and the Soviet Union.

Stalin was a ruthless dictator responsible for the imprisonment or death of many millions of people. It is estimated that as many as twenty million Soviet citizens died as a result of his policies. Nevertheless, he gained a reputation as a great war leader, guiding the Soviet Union to victory over the Germans in World War II.

Stalin had villages and towns named after himself. He accepted titles such as "Father of Nations" and "Gardener of Human Happiness." He also had Soviet history falsely rewritten to make it seem that he played a more important role in establishing communism in the Russian Empire than he actually did during the revolution and afterward. The most famous Georgian in world history died in 1953.

In 1918, the Social Democratic Party of Georgia established the short-lived Democratic Republic of Georgia, an independent country. For the first time in 117 years, Georgia was not under Russian control. In February

1921, however, following victories throughout the former Russian Empire, the Red Army marched into Georgia, driving the leaders of the Social Democratic party into exile. Georgia was once more in the grip of its powerful neighbor. Along with the Red Army came two important Georgian communists—Grigory Ordzhonikidze and Joseph Stalin—to establish communist control. In 1923, the communist government in Moscow formed the Union of Soviet Socialist Republics (USSR) or Soviet Union. The Soviet Union consisted of republics and **autonomous** regions.

Stalin and Beria

Georgia was established as a Soviet republic (similar to a U.S. state) along with Armenia and Azerbaijan, inside the Transcaucasian Soviet Federated Socialist Republic (SFSR), a part of the Soviet Union. The Georgian Social Democrats, still popular despite their earlier defeat, organized a rebellion in 1924 that Stalin, who was now head of the Communist Party of the Soviet Union, brutally squashed. He ordered the execution of five thousand people, firmly establishing Soviet rule in Georgia. Stalin was helped in his rule of Georgia by a fellow Georgian, Lavrenty Beria (1899–1953).

In 1928, Stalin took control of the Soviet Union. He established a dictatorship that would last until his death in 1953. Stalin appointed Beria as communist head of Georgia in 1931. In 1936, Stalin dissolved the Transcaucasian

Joseph Stalin (third from right), *along with members of the Russian Communist Party, addresses crowds from atop the Lenin Mausoleum in Moscow's Red Square in November 1926.*

SFSR and made Georgia one of the fifteen republics of the Soviet Union.

During Stalin's dictatorship, peasant farmers were forced to join large collective farms. Those who refused were imprisoned or executed. Even after Beria was called to Moscow to head the Soviet Union's secret police, he and Stalin kept tight control on Georgia.

During World War II (1939–1945), the Georgians helped defend the Soviet Union against the German invasion of the northern Caucasus. German paratroopers were dropped into Georgia to help the advance of the main German invasion force, but were promptly caught by the local **militia**. In all, the Soviet Union is estimated to have lost more than twenty million people as a result of the war, and 300,000 Georgians paid with their lives.

By the end of the war, Stalin's policies had converted Georgia from mainly a farming society into an industrial society based in cities. All industry and agriculture under the Soviet system were supposed to be owned by the government. Georgians, however, developed many ways to build a flourishing "second economy," providing goods and services not available in the planned state economy. Far from the center of power in Moscow, the Georgians were able to grow their own crops privately and run their own cottage industries.

Collective Farms

A collective farm was a large government-run farm that combined the land of many smaller private farms. In 1929, Stalin began a program to modernize Soviet agriculture by consolidating small farms into large parcels that could be farmed using tractors and other modern equipment.

In 1931, the head of the Communist Party in Georgia, Mikheil Kakhiani, ordered an all-out campaign to collectivize Georgian farmers. Many farmers resisted the move to state-run farms, however, by slaughtering their cattle, smashing their farm tools, and burning their fields. Many of those resisters were deported to Siberia, the Soviet Union's vast northern wilderness. By the mid-1930s, the resistance had diminished, and most farming in Georgia was done by collective farms. Collective farms, however, were never successful. Throughout much of its history, the Soviet Union was plagued by food shortages. Even before the collapse of the Soviet Union, the **collectivization** of farming was phased out in Georgia and in the other Soviet republics.

Gorbachev's Reforms

In the late 1980s, the Soviet Union underwent political and social changes under the leadership of Mikhail Gorbachev (b. 1931). In the new atmosphere of glasnost (openness), Gorbachev promoted more freedom within the Soviet system.

In April 1989, however, demonstrations in Tbilisi to demand independence were brutally suppressed by Soviet special troops. Twenty civilians were killed. After the event, Gorbachev said that he had not ordered the shooting and that the decision had been made by local commanders. Nevertheless, the incident led to increased pressure on the Georgian Communist Party to give up power.

New political parties appeared in Georgia and were not banned by the Soviets. Free elections held in 1990 were won by a **coalition** called the Round Table, led by Zviad Gamsakhurdia (1939–1994).

Outside of Georgia, political and economic troubles were building up within the whole Soviet Union. Loud voices demanded an end to rule by the Communist Party and more power for the individual republics. The loudest voice of all was that of Boris Yeltsin, who was elected head of the Russian Soviet Federated Socialist Republic (RSFSR). On June 12, 1990, the legislature of the RSFSR, led by Yeltsin, voted to declare itself independent of the Soviet Union. In July, Yeltsin quit the Communist Party.

It was the beginning of the end for the Soviet Union. On August 18, 1991, a group of dedicated communists led a **coup** against Gorbachev. The Soviet leader was held under house arrest in the Crimea, the area of the southern Soviet Union where he was vacationing. Yeltsin rushed to his presidential offices in Moscow in defiance of the coup leaders. Soldiers supporting the coup defected to Yeltsin, and Gorbachev was rescued and returned to Moscow. Gorbachev was safe, but the Soviet Union was finished. In November 1991, Yeltsin issued a decree banning the Communist Party throughout the RSFSR and declaring Russian independence.

One by one, the other republics that made up the Soviet Union followed Yeltsin's lead and declared independence. Georgia made its declaration on April 9, 1991. On December 25, Gorbachev resigned as president of the Soviet Union. On December 31, the Soviet flag was lowered for the last time over the Kremlin, the once-feared center of Soviet power. Georgia and the other former Soviet republics now faced the world as independent nations.

CHAPTER 4

Struggles for Independence

The first elected president of the new Georgian republic was Zviad Gamsakhurdia, the leader of the Round Table coalition. Almost immediately, he was hit with charges that his government suppressed freedoms. His opponents launched a violent attempt to overthrow his government, attacking a number of government buildings in Tbilisi. Heavy fighting continued in Tbilisi until January 6, 1992, when Gamsakhurdia and members of his government escaped and made their way to safety in Armenia. He was replaced by a military council that soon handed power over to Eduard Shevardnadze (b. 1928). Shevardnadze had served as Soviet foreign minister under Gorbachev.

Gamsakhurdia, however, returned to western Georgia in 1993 to lead a rebellion against Shevardnadze. Shevardnadze, with Russian help, destroyed Gamsakhurdia's poorly armed supporters. The ousted president was later reported dead.

Georgia under Shevardnadze

In 1995, Georgians voted on a new constitution that strengthened the powers of the presidency and elected

Georgian president Eduard Shevardnadze, speaking at a cabinet meeting in Tbilisi in February 1998, defended his administration against charges of corruption and repression.

Shevardnadze for a five-year term as president. He received 75 percent of the vote. Shevardnadze's party, the Citizens' Union of Georgia (CUG), also won 107 of parliament's 231 seats.

Shevardnadze's government became increasingly associated with widespread corruption that slowed Georgia's economic growth. Two Russian-supported breakaway regions (Abkhazia and South Ossetia) remained outside the control of the Tbilisi government, and the republic of Ajaria was ruled by separatist leader Aslan Abswahidze. Shevardnadze was also widely criticized for clamping down on the freedoms Georgians had been promised in their new constitution.

In 1998, the U.S. State Department released a document saying that freedom of the press, considered a fundamental right in a democracy, was being squashed in Shevardnadze's Georgia. There were stories of reporters' video- and audiotapes being destroyed by government officials, and a climate of growing fear.

In September 1997, the government put on trial a newspaper reporter who wrote about corruption in a part of Abkhazia controlled by Georgian troops. Critics charge that the government pressured the court to find the journalist guilty. Shevardnadze was widely accused of using the police to clamp down on Georgia's media. In a 1998 speech, he is quoted as saying that, in a conflict between the police and the press, "the police are the main support of the state."

60 Minutes, Georgian Style

In the mid-1990s, according to *Global Journalist* magazine, Akaki Gogichaishvili, a Georgian, and Andrei Babitsky, a Russian, were studying in the United States. Inspired by the American TV show *60 Minutes*, they decided to do a Georgian version of the show. Their show, also called *60 Minutes*, aired in Georgia in December 1997. They covered controversial material about the Shevardnadze government.

Week after week, the show broadcast details of the corruption of high officials and of friends and family of President Shevardnadze. In May 1998 Gogichaishvili got a call from Georgia's deputy general prosecutor. If Gogichaishvili did not leave the country, he would be killed, the prosecutor said. The prosecutor later denied that he had made such a threat.

Instead of fleeing, Gogichaishvili held a press conference to tell about the threat. Soon, demonstrators were parading in front of Shevardnadze's office, insisting that the president guarantee Gogichaishvili's safety. Shevardnadze eventually did.

Freedom of the press is a major principle in the United States and in other democratic societies. In the United States, this freedom is enshrined in the First Amendment to the Constitution. In part, the Amendment states, "Congress shall make no law...abridging the freedom of speech, or of the press." Freedom of speech is often called the First Freedom because it is so essential to democracy. If there were not a First Amendment, a law could be passed, for example, saying that anyone who criticizes the president could be punished by being thrown into jail.

In modern democracies, such as those in the United States and Europe, the press has acted as a kind "super voice" of the people. It has called attention to corruption, fraud, abuse, incompetence, and misuse of power at all levels of government. Although Georgia's constitution guarantees freedom of the press, the spirit of press freedom has been lacking, especially under Shevardnadze's rule. Media outlets that are seen as unfavorable to the government often find access difficult or impossible. In that way, independence of the press, which is important for press freedom, has been limited in Georgia.

60 Minutes remained on the air, but Gogichaishvili remained pessimistic about Georgia's future. "I don't think my programs will bring changes," he told *Global Journalist*, "but I think I should keep on doing it—just in case."

In 2000, Shevardnadze was reelected with nearly 80 percent of the vote, but there were **allegations** of widespread voter fraud.

Discontent reached its peak just after the parliamentary elections of November 2, 2003. The election results, which gave a victory to Shevardnadze's party, were denounced by local and international observers as being rigged. Mikhail Saakashvili, a thirty-five-year-old, U.S.-educated former justice minister, claimed that his party had actually won the elections. His claim was supported by independent exit polls. He urged Georgians to demonstrate against Shevardnadze in a show of non-violent civil disobedience.

The Rose Revolution

In mid-November 2003, massive antigovernment demonstrations sparked by the election began in almost all major cities and towns in Georgia. The opposition protest reached its peak on November 22, the day of the opening session of the new parliament, which the protesters considered illegitimate.

On November 23, following a week of street protests, thousands of demonstrators, led by Saakashvili, forced their way through the thick wooden doors of the parliament building to find Shevardnadze giving a speech inside. Saakashvili held a long-stemmed red rose above his head and shouted "Resign!" Shevardnadze was rushed by his bodyguards out of the parliament building by a back door.

After the confrontation in parliament, tens of thousands of demonstrators took to the streets to protest the flawed results of a parliamentary election. Shevardnadze sent hundreds of soldiers into the streets of Tbilisi. Student demonstrators started handing out red roses to the soldiers. Many soldiers laid down their guns. "People were kissing the police and military, it was really spectacular," Giorgi Kandelaki, a student, told the BBC.

On November 23, Shevardnadze resigned and was put under house arrest. As of April 2006, he was still confined to his house. More than 100,000 people celebrated the resignation all night long. During the Rose Revolution, not one person was injured, and not a drop of blood was spilled.

In January 2004, Saakashvili was elected president. The following

A young Georgian boy carries firewood for heat at a market in Tbilisi in January 2006, as freezing temperatures blanketed the capital of Georgia. The cold snap added to the misery of those living in this mountainous region because a Russian pipeline exploded and caused a major power line break. This natural gas shortage cut electricity to millions of Georgians.

month, the Georgian parliament passed constitutional amendments. The new amendments strengthened the president at the expense of parliament. They also gave the country a cabinet and a prime minister for the first time. In the first year after the revolution, dozens of former government officials were jailed on corruption and **embezzlement** charges.

CHAPTER 5

Troubled Region

A map of the Caucasus Mountains region showing ethnic, cultural, and religious boundaries looks like a crazy quilt. It is an area the size of California with dozens of nationalities, each with its own history, culture, religion, language, and, often, hatred of the other nationalities.

When the Soviet Union dissolved in 1991, these nationalities were contained in four nations: Russia, Georgia, Armenia, and Azerbaijan. The major challenge for all four nations since independence has been to keep their various nationalities and ethnic groups from separating to form their own tiny nations.

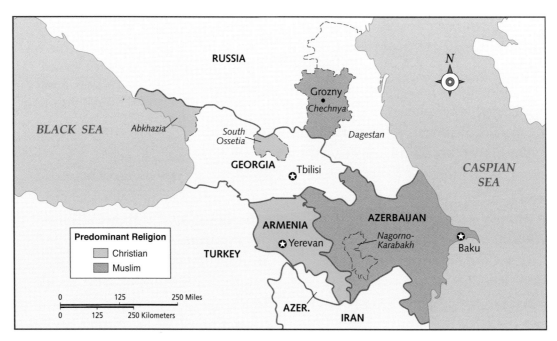

A map of the Caucasus Mountains region illustrates the ethnic differences between bordering nations.

In addition to the ongoing conflicts in Abkhazia and South Ossetia in Georgia, two major ethnic and nationalist conflicts keep the entire region in turmoil. One is the rebellion in Chechnya, a region of southern Russia. The other is an ethnic conflict in Nagorno-Karabakh, part of Azerbaijan.

The Chechen War

Chechnya, a province of Russia on Russia's southern border next to Georgia, has been a problem for the Russian government for hundreds of years. In the nineteenth century, it took Russian armies more than fifty years—to 1859—to take control of Chechnya from Muslim fighters led by Imam Shamil. The Chechens, who are mainly Muslims, lived uneasily under the czars and, later, under Soviet rule. At the end of World War II, Stalin sought **vengeance** against the Chechens because some Chechen rebel forces helped the Germans in their invasion of the Soviet Union. He deported much of Chechnya's population to the wastes of Siberia and the empty plains of Central Asia. The Chechens were allowed to return only in 1957.

When the Soviet Union collapsed in 1991, the Chechens looked to achieve their long-awaited independence from Russian domination. Dzhokhar Dudayev, a Chechen and a senior officer in the Soviet air force, declared

Chechen separatist leader Dzhokhar Dudayev, killed in 1996 in a missile attack in southwestern Chechnya, is shown in this photograph taken in December 1994 as he visited the town of Ordzhonikidzevskaya, 28 miles (45 km) west of the capital city of Grozny.

Chechnya an independent nation. For three years, Russian leader Boris Yeltsin tried to keep Chechnya in the Russian Federation by diplomacy. Dudayev, however, became increasingly more defiant of Moscow and continued to arm Chechen fighters.

Fierce Resistance

In December 1994, Yeltsin sent the Russian army into Chechnya to get rid of Dudayev and his supporters. Yeltsin thought he would have a quick victory against the rebels. He was wrong. The

A Chechen woman walks through the deserted and destroyed capital city of Grozny, still held by a few thousand Chechens fighting off the Russian military in August 1996.

Chechens put up a fierce resistance, and the death toll on both sides rose. Up to 100,000 people—many of them civilians—were killed in the nearly two years of war that followed. Grozny, Chechnya's capital, was flattened and destroyed. In June 1995, Chechen rebels seized hundreds of Russian hostages at a hospital. More than a hundred were killed when Russian commandos raided the hospital. In 1996, Dudayev was killed in a Russian missile attack.

In 1996, Russia and Chechen rebels signed a peace agreement giving Chechnya self-rule within Russia, but not independence. The main rebel army commander, Aslan Maskhadov, was elected president of the Chechen Republic. By August 1996, Chechen rebels supporting full independence launched an attack on Russian troops in Grozny. Russian troops agreed to withdraw. In May 1997, Yeltsin and Maskhadov signed a formal peace treaty.

Expansion of the War

Instead of enjoying peace after the agreement, Chechnya continued in turmoil and bloodshed. The Russians failed to spend money to rebuild Chechnya's shattered cities. Brutal Chechen warlords grew rich through organized crime and kidnapping. Murder and robberies took place every day. In March 1999, the top Russian official in Chechnya was kidnapped by Chechen rebels and murdered. Amid growing lawlessness, Maskhadov imposed a state of emergency.

In August 1999, Chechen fighters crossed into the Russian republic of Dagestan. The raid was part of a **jihad** to establish an independent Islamic state in Dagestan and Chechnya. The fighters called upon Muslims around the world to fight Russia in the name of Islam.

Vladimir Putin was the leader of Russia. He vowed a renewed war to destroy the Chechen rebels. In late summer a series of terrorist bombings inside Russia killed hundreds of people. In October, with the Russian army on the move into Chechnya, 200,000 civilians fled Chechnya for neighboring republics. By February 2000, the Russians had recaptured Grozny and leveled what was left of the city.

The war continued into 2001 and 2002. Putin accused the rebels of being in contact with international terrorists. In August 2002, Georgia accused Russia of conducting air raids close to the border that divides Georgia from Chechnya. In 2003, the Chechen war still raged off and on, with terror attacks by the Chechen rebels hitting deep inside Russia itself. In September 2004, hundreds of children were killed or wounded when Chechens captured a Russian school and held the children hostage. In February 2006, a dozen Russian soldiers died in an explosion at Russian military barracks near Grozny.

A Landlocked Nation

The Republic of Armenia is a nation the size of Maryland with a population of three million people. It lies between Georgia and Azerbaijan. Armenia is the only completely landlocked nation in the Caucasus region. Like Georgia, Armenia is a Christian nation surrounded by Islamic nations. It is also a nation with a long cultural tradition and ancient heritage. Armenia was part of the Roman Empire and converted to Christianity thirty years before Georgia did, becoming the first nation in the world to adopt Christianity as its state religion.

Modern Armenia comprises only a small part of ancient Armenia, one of the world's oldest centers of civilization. In the third and fourth centuries A.D. Armenia stretched from the Black

In remembrance of the massacre of 1.5 million Armenians by Ottoman Turks during World War I, Archbishop Mesrob Ashjian of the Armenian Apostolic Church of New York blesses a memorial statue outside a church in Ridgefield, New Jersey, on April 20, 1997. The day marked the eighty-second anniversary of the Armenian massacre. Joining the archbishop are Souren Papazian (left), a survivor of the attack, and Mrs. Keghanoush Kinossian, the wife of a survivor.

and 1.5 million Armenians were killed by the Turks. The Armenians say this was **genocide**, a deliberate attempt by the Turks to wipe the Armenians out as a people. The Turks claim that the deaths were the result of a civil war, combined with disease and famine. Each year, on April 24, Armenians all around the world, including 385,000 U.S. citizens of Armenian ancestry, remember the attempted genocide in Armenia. Even today, Armenia and Turkey have no diplomatic relations.

Political Problems

Like Georgia, Armenia was once a republic inside the Soviet Union. Also like Georgia, Armenia has had its political and economic struggles as an independent nation since the end of the Soviet Union. The histories of the two nations have been marked by political instability.

The stated goal of Armenia's government has been to build a European-style parliamentary democracy. As in Georgia, however, international observers have often questioned the fairness of Armenia's parliamentary and presidential elections. Levon Ter-Petrossian became president of Armenia in 1991, shortly after independence. In 1996, he was reelected, but had to send tanks into the streets of Yerevan, Armenia's capital, because of widespread allegations of election

Sea to the Caspian Sea and included much of today's Georgia.

Between 1915 and 1918, when Armenia was part of the Turkish Ottoman Empire, between 650,000

fraud. By January 1998, growing demonstrations against Ter-Petrossian's dictatorial rule forced his resignation. Robert Kocharian was elected president. In 1999, gunmen opened fire in the Armenian parliament, killing the prime minister, the parliamentary Speaker, and six other officials. The gunmen accused the government of leading Armenia into political and economic ruin.

Kocharian won a second term as president in 2003 amid further allegations of election fraud and ballot stuffing. In the last few years, however, there have been fewer demonstrations and incidents of violence, although allegations of voter fraud and corruption still plague the government.

Unemployment and poverty in Armenia today are widespread, but the situation is improved from a few years ago. Tourism, which has developed into a major industry, is one economic bright spot. In 2005, about 318,000 tourists visited Armenia, compared to 45,000 in 2004. While reforms have improved economic growth in the last several years, Armenia's economy still has problems lifting the living standards of the people. Over the last ten years, the country lost about one-third of its population as young Armenians left to find a better life in other countries.

The United States is a major ally of Armenia. At the end of 2005, the United States gave Armenia a $235 million grant to help eliminate rural poverty. In announcing the grant, U.S. secretary of state Condoleezza Rice said that it "will empower Armenian men and women to better their own lives, to strengthen their own communities and to transform their lives." Secretary Rice said that the money will improve the lives of 750,000 Armenians, three-quarters of the country's rural population.

Muslim Azerbaijan

Azerbaijan, a country slightly larger in land area than the state of Utah, is

A Muslim man, shadowed by oil rigs in the background, prays in Baku, Azerbaijan, in November 2005.

Armenia's neighbor to the northeast. Unlike Armenia, Azerbaijan has a coastline. It fronts the Caspian Sea. Azerbaijan, unlike Georgia and Armenia, is a Muslim nation. Ninety-three percent of its people are Muslims with strong ties to Iran. The main ethnic group in the country is the Azeris.

Azerbaijan was acquired by the Russian empire from Persia (the ancient name for Iran) through two treaties in 1813 and 1828. Like Georgia and Armenia, it became a Soviet republic and, in 1991, an independent nation when the Soviet Union collapsed. Also like Georgia and Armenia, Azerbaijan has been plagued by political unrest, riots, and charges of election fraud. The president of Azerbaijan is Illham Aliyev, who ran for president when his father, Heydar Aliyev, the former president, died in 2003. Heydar Aliyev had run Azerbaijan with an iron fist since independence.

Illham Aliyev won the 2003 presidential election by a landslide. European observers, however, said that the election had been hurt by voter intimidation, violence, and unfair reporting by the government-run press. Many antigovernment demonstrations were met with police violence and many arrests.

Azerbaijan's economy, which is based mainly on industry, is growing at a rapid rate. In 2005, the economy grew by 11 percent, mainly because of oil. Azerbaijan has large oil deposits near its Caspian Sea coast. Western countries have invested millions in the development of the country's oil and gas reserves. In 2005, a new oil pipeline opened, running from Azerbaijan through Georgia to the Turkish port of Ceyhan, boosting Azerbaijan's output of oil. This oil pipeline has increased Georgia's strategic value in the world.

Even though oil has brought riches to Azerbaijan, the wealth has not reached all the people. There are large pockets of extreme poverty in the country, say experts.

Azerbaijan versus Armenia

Even though Azerbaijan and Armenia are neighbors, they are not friends. In fact, the two nations have been close to war in recent years. The problem lies in Nagorno-Karabakh, a region just east of Armenia, inside Azerbaijan, that has a mainly Armenian population.

While the region was still part of the Soviet Union, Armenian discontent with the Azeris exploded into armed conflict. In 1988 and 1989, Azeris fled Nagorno-Karabakh, while Armenians fled into Nagorno-Karabakh from the rest of Azerbaijan.

In 1991, when the Soviet Union collapsed, the Armenian population

An elderly woman looks out from her straw shelter at a refugee camp in central Azerbaijan in October 1997. Thousands have been displaced as a result of the war in the Armenian-population region of Nagorno-Karabakh in Azerbaijan.

of Nagorno-Karabakh declared Nagorno-Karabakh an independent republic. Fighting again broke out. Backed by the government and troops of Armenia, the Armenians took control of the region and some surrounding territory.

With the help of the Russians, both sides signed a cease-fire in 1994, leaving Nagorno-Karabakh under the **de facto** control of the rebel Armenian government there. No final settlement has yet been signed, although Russia, France, and the United States continue to sponsor peace talks to settle the issue. The conflict over this region has prevented any real cooperation between Armenia and Azerbaijan, causing tensions that some fear could eventually plunge the whole region into war. It is estimated that between twenty thousand and thirty thousand people lost their lives during the conflict. More than one million fled from their homes.

CHAPTER 6

Is the Rose Revolution Wilting?

On March 8, 2006, there were signs that the Rose Revolution in Georgia, once so full of promise, was wilting.

Thousands of people took to the streets of Tbilisi in the biggest antigovernment demonstration since Mikhail Saakashvili came to power in the Rose Revolution. Eight thousand people gathered outside the Georgian parliament building to demand that Saakashvili resign. The cause this time was not a disputed election. It was a general feeling among the people, and particularly among opposition parties, that Saakashvili has not followed through on his two campaign promises. One was to improve Georgia's economy. The other was to bring the two breakaway regions of Abkhazia and South Ossetia back under Georgian control.

"The president said food prices have risen only a little; but this is not true," protester Tamriko Georgadze told a reporter for the Associated Press. "For meat, which I cannot

A Georgian protester holds up an altered picture of Georgian president Mikhail Saakashvili as demonstrators call for his resignation in front of the parliament building in Tbilisi in March 2006. The poster depicts Saakashvili wearing a moustache akin to Adolf Hitler's, comparing the current president to the late German dictator.

Mikhail Saakashvili, who was born on December 21, 1967, in Tbilisi, has a strong U.S. and European connection. After graduating from the School of International Law of the Kiev (Ukraine) State University and working briefly for the Georgian government, he received a grant from the U.S. State Department to study in the United States.

He received two law degrees in the United States, one from Columbia University in New York in 1994 and the second from George Washington University in Washington, D.C., in 1995. Also in 1995, he received a diploma from the International Institute of Human Rights in Strasbourg, France.

After graduation, Saakashvili stayed in the United States and worked for the New York law firm of Patterson, Belknap, Webb & Tyler. He was approached by an old friend who was in the United States to recruit talented young Georgians to enter politics. In December 1995, Saakashvili ran for a seat in the Georgian parliament, representing the Union of Citizens of Georgia, Shevardnadze's party. He won.

Once in parliament, Saakashvili made a name for himself as chair of a parliamentary committee concerned with election reform. He generated a lot of press attention and appeared on television. Soon polls found him to be the second most popular person in Georgia, behind Shevardnadze. He was even named "man of the year" by a panel of journalists.

On October 12, 2000, Shevardnadze appointed Saakashvili minister of justice, a position similar to the U.S. attorney general's. He started major reforms of the Georgian criminal justice and prison systems, but on September 5, 2001, he resigned, appalled at the corruption in Shevardnadze's government. "I consider it immoral for me to remain as a member of Shevardnadze's government," he told Georgian television. He declared that corruption had penetrated to the core of Georgia's government and that Shevardnadze lacked the will to deal with it. He said that "current developments" would turn Georgia into a "criminal enclave" in one or two years.

He left the government and formed an opposition political party, the United National Movement. After he forced Shevardnadze's resignation in the Rose Revolution, Saakashvili was elected president by 96 percent of the vote in 2004. At age thirty-six, he became the youngest head of government in Europe.

Workers take apart a Russian military tank at a plant in Tbilisi in September 2000 as part of the withdrawal effort of the Russian military in Georgia. Russia kept tanks and artillery at four bases in Georgia after the collapse of the Soviet Union in 1991. A 1999 agreement calls for their withdrawal from two of those bases by July 2001.

afford to buy for my children, the price has nearly doubled in two years. I have never been involved in politics, but now I am against the current authorities."

On March 29, more than seven thousand Georgians again demonstrated in Tbilisi, calling for the president to resign. "We have brought the current government to power, and now we must push it to resign," said Zviad Dzidziguri, an opposition party leader who played an active part in the Rose Revolution.

"The sooner we replace this government, the better it will be for our people," said Konstantine Gamsakhurdia, son of Georgia's late president and leader of a small opposition party.

Rising Tensions

In the spring of 2006, tensions between Georgia and Russia continued to rise. In February, the Georgian parliament adopted a resolution aimed at expelling Russian peacekeepers from South Ossetia. In March, a high-ranking Russian official, Gennady

Bukayev, reportedly said that the Russian government was already considering annexing South Ossetia. The statement angered the Georgian government. "Tbilisi regards such irresponsible statements by a high-ranking Russian governmental official...[as] totally unacceptable," the Georgian Foreign Ministry's press service said in a press release.

In Abkhazia, things were not much better. On March 7, 2006, four Abkhazians, including a seven-year-old girl, were shot dead. Abkhazian authorities accused Georgia of being behind the killings, which were blamed on Georgian-supported terrorists. "The killing of four civilians... in Abkhazia...is pure terrorism and official Tbilisi is behind this crime," Abkhazian separatist leader Sergei Bagapsh is quoted as saying by Russia's Interfax news agency.

On March 9, the foreign minister of Abkhazia hardened the breakaway region's position on ever rejoining Georgia. "Abkhazia has legal, historical, and moral grounds to reject Georgia's [authority]," he said. "Permanent genocide and ethnic cleansing against the Abkhaz people give us full grounds to turn down... Georgia." The foreign minister continued, "Abkhazia has been an independent state for thirteen years now. We won our independence by sacrific-

ing the lives of many young people on the altar of freedom.... There is no way, no pressure that will make us surrender our achievements.... No force can make us go back to become part of Georgia, despite the opinions of senators, deputies and other persons."

On March 29, the Georgian ambassador to the UN accused Russia of trying to destroy the integrity of the Georgian state and seeking Abkhazia's **secession** from Georgia. Although he stated that Georgia would never agree to that, he stressed that the country was committed to a peaceful resolution to the conflict.

Amid these developments, fears of war between Russia and Georgia over the breakaway provinces were rising both in Georgia and in Russia. Andrey Dobrov, a respected Russian television commentator, said that Russia would be placed in a very difficult position if Georgia uses military force to retake South Ossetia and Abkhazia. Russian intervention to help either of these regions, he said, would be seen by the West as aggression against Georgia, while standing idly by would suggest that Russia is not capable of holding together its troublesome southern regions.

On March 31, however, relations between Georgia and Russia warmed a little when the two countries signed an agreement for the withdrawal of

In the breakaway Georgian region of Abkhazia, supporters of opposition presidential candidate Sergei Bagapsh celebrate the seizure of outgoing President Vladislav Ardzinba's office in November 2004.

most of the Russian military bases from Georgia. Two Russian military bases were left in the country: one near the city of Akhalkalaki and the other at the Black Sea port of Batumi. About three thousand Russian troops were stationed at the two bases, which are holdovers from the Soviet era. The withdrawals are to be completed by 2008. It was a "historic day for Georgia as we signed an agreement putting an end to the 200-year stay of Russian forces on the territory of Georgia," said Georgian deputy defense minister Mamuka Kudava.

Some Optimism

Despite growing opposition to his rule, Georgian president Mikhail Saakashvili remains optimistic about his country's future. In a televised press conference on March 16, 2006, he rejected charges that Georgia is facing major economic problems. He said that the government is rebuilding the country's infrastructure and delivering improved public services, and is even on its way to joining the North Atlantic Treaty Organization (NATO).

"By the end of 2008, we will have a modern health service that meets

European standards, a modern education system that meets European standards, a modern transport system that meets European standards…and we will be members of NATO," he said. "We will be members of the North Atlantic Alliance. Georgia is gaining international respect," he added. (North Atlantic Alliance is another name for NATO.)

"We will become a modern country," he had said in an earlier speech. "We are building roads, hydroelectric power stations and the energy sector. In a word, we are starting to resemble a real, normal, civilized country. Time is needed for that. If I had a magic wand, I would wave it and this road would be ready in a day, but I do not have such a wand. Instead of a wand, we have a large amount of equipment, which you can see here, we have many very good workers, honest, hardworking people who will work day and night to rebuild Georgia and make it a successful country."

The question remains, however, how long the Georgian people will give their president to make good on his promises.

NATO

The North Atlantic Treaty Organization was established by a 1949 treaty signed by twelve nations: Belgium, Canada, Denmark, France, Iceland, Italy, Luxembourg, the Netherlands, Norway, Portugal, the United Kingdom, and the United States. Greece and Turkey joined in 1952, Germany in 1955, and Spain in 1982. Poland, the Czech Republic, and Hungary joined in 1999. Nations that sign the treaty commit themselves to treat an armed attack on any one of them as an attack on all. They agree to defend with military force any member that is attacked. Originally, NATO was formed to defend Western Europe against an attack by the Soviet Union or its allies. When the Soviet Union collapsed, some former Soviet allies, such as Poland and the Czech Republic, joined NATO. If Georgia succeeds in joining NATO in 2008, it would be a boost to the country's attempts to prevent Russian military help to rebels in Abkhazia and North Ossetia, which could be interpreted as an attack on all the NATO nations. Becoming a member of NATO would also greatly increase Georgia's standing in the world. It would mean that Georgia was accepted by Europe and the United States as a modern democratic nation.

Time Line

2100–1500 B.C.	Trialeti culture flourishes.
300s B.C.	The kingdom of Iberia is established.
66 B.C.	Georgia becomes part of the Roman Empire.
A.D. 330	Georgia adopts Christianity.
645	Arabs capture Tbilisi.
813	Ashot I assumes the throne of Georgia.
1073–1125	The reign of David the Builder.
1160–1213	The reign of Queen Tamar.
1220	Mongols invade Georgia.
1801	Georgia becomes part of the Russian Empire.
1918	Independent Georgian state is declared.
1921	Georgia is declared a Soviet Socialist Republic.
1922	Georgia becomes a founding member of the Soviet Union.
1928	Joseph Stalin, from Georgia, becomes Soviet leader.
1936	Georgia becomes a full republic of the Soviet Union.
1990	Georgian forces fight separatists in South Ossetia.
1991	Georgia becomes an independent nation; Zviad Gamsakhurdia is elected president.
1992	Eduard Shevardnadze becomes Georgian leader.
1993	Abkhazia declares itself independent from Georgia.
1995	Georgians approve a new constitution; Shevardnadze becomes president.
2003	The Rose Revolution forces Shevardnadze to resign.
2004	Mikhail Saakashvili wins presidential election.
2005	January: South Ossetia demands full independence; May: President George W. Bush becomes the first U.S. leader to visit Georgia.
2006	January: Explosions on the Russian side of the border damage section of gas pipeline; April: Georgia and Russia sign an agreement to eliminate Russian military bases in Georgia by 2008.

Glossary

allegations charges against a person

annals records of events by year

archaeologists people who study past human life and culture

autonomous having self-rule but not complete independence

breakaway seeking to sever an alliance with another state

cease-fire a truce suspending hostilities

coalition a temporary alliance

collectivization group ownership of property

communism belief that all property should be owned in common, usually by the government

coup sudden action to obtain power

de facto existing in fact

dynasty a **succession** of rulers who belong to the same family

embezzlement taking money or property illegally

ethnic term applied to a group of people who share a cultural and/or religious heritage

ethnic cleansing forced removal of a whole ethnic group from its land

genocide deliberate killing of a whole race or religious or ethnic group

infrastructure a nation's roads, bridges, airports, and other public structures

intellectuals people motivated mainly by ideas

jihad Muslim holy war

legislature an elected or selected body of people responsible for making laws for a state or nation

militia unofficial group of fighters

Mongols people related to the main population of Mongolia

nationalism devotion to the interests of one's nation

peacekeepers a military force whose presence aids in securing peace in a region

protectorate a weak country that is under the official protection and partial control of a stronger country

radicals people who want revolutionary change in a country or system

refugees people who flee a country in times of persecution

secession the withdrawal of one political entity from another

separatists people who advocate political separation from another state

sorcerer magician

sovereignty state of independence

stalemate a situation in which no further action can be taken because of a failure of two parties to agree

succession the order in which one person follows another to ascend a throne or political office

unification consolidation into one nation

United Nations (UN) an international organization founded to promote peace, security, and economic development around the world

vengeance retaliation for harm or injury

viceroy a person governing a colony or province as representative of a king or emperor

For More Information

Books

Kaeter, Margaret, and Burke, Justin. *The Caucasian Republics.* Facts
    On File, 2004.

Kasbarian, Lucine. *Armenia: A Rugged Land, an Enduring People.* Dillon
    Press/Silver Burdett, 1997.

Pavloic, Zoran, and Gritzner, Charles F. *Republic of Georgia.* Chelsea
    House, 2005.

Streissguth, Thomas. *The Transcaucasus.* Lucent Books, 2001.

Web Sites

sisauri.tripod.com/ref/cuisine/cuisine.html
    Georgian food with recipes

www.abkhazia.org/home.html
    Information about Abkhazia from a separatist Web site

www.eurasianet.org/resource/georgia/index.shtml
    Latest news from Georgia through a European Web site

www.odci.gov/cia/publications/factbook/geos/gg.html|
    Up-to-date facts about Georgia from the Central Intelligence Agency

www.oneworldjourneys.com/georgia/0419_notebook_1.html
    Slide shows of the region

www.state.gov/r/pa/ei/bgn/5253.htm
    The most up-to-date information about Georgia from the U.S. Department
    of State Fact Book

Publisher's note to educators and parents: Our editors have carefully
reviewed these Web sites to ensure that they are suitable for children.
  Many Web sites change frequently, however, and we cannot guarantee
that a site's future contents will continue to meet our high standards
of quality and educational value. Be advised that children should be
closely supervised whenever they access the Internet.

Index

About the Author

Charles Piddock is a former editor in chief of Weekly Reader Corporation, publisher of sixteen classroom magazines for schools from pre-K through high school, including *Current Events, Current Science,* and *Teen Newsweek.* In his career with Weekly Reader, he has written and edited hundreds of articles for young people of all ages on world and national affairs, science, literature, and other topics. Before working at Weekly Reader, he worked in publishing in New York City and, before that, served as a Peace Corps volunteer in rural West Bengal, India.